Ganesha's Whispers

Tales of Wisdom and Beginnings

GANESHA'S WHISPERS - TALES OF WISDOM AND BEGINNINGS

First edition. November 12, 2023.

Copyright © 2023 JIGNESH SAPRA.

ISBN: 979-8223910787

Written by JIGNESH SAPRA.

Table of Contents

About the Book

Embark on a journey into the heart of diverse communities, where individuals face challenges that test the limits of their resilience. **"Ganesha's Whispers: Tales of Wisdom and Beginnings"** weaves a tapestry of inspiring stories that delve into the intricate dance of life, showcasing the strength of the human spirit and the guiding whispers of the divine.

As the stories unfold, a common thread emerges — the power of resilience, community cooperation, and the belief in divine intervention. Each tale unfolds a unique chapter, contributing to the harmony of their respective worlds. The characters, guided by whispers of divinity, become beacons of inspiration for readers seeking solace, strength, and a renewed sense of hope.

" **Ganesha's Whispers** " is more than a collection of stories; it's a testament to the indomitable spirit of humanity and the transformative power of collective resilience. Join us on this literary odyssey, where the pages resonate with the echoes of challenges overcome, innovative solutions found, and the harmonious rhythm of communities united by a shared journey.

Open the book and listen closely; you might just hear the whispers of divinity guiding you through the tales of resilience and harmony within.

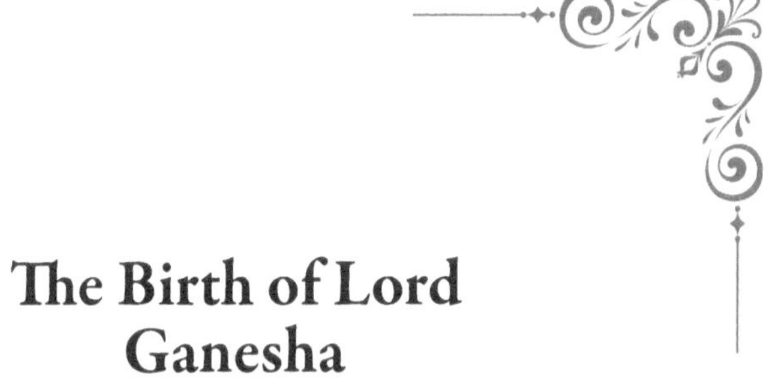

The Birth of Lord Ganesha

In ancient times, in the heavenly abode of Lord Shiva and Goddess Parvati, there lived an atmosphere of serenity and divine harmony. The couple was deeply in love, and they often spent time together in meditation and contemplation. However, their longing for a child grew stronger with each passing day.

One day, as Parvati was preparing for a ritual bath, she decided to create a son from the turmeric paste she was using. She molded the paste into a beautiful form and, with her divine powers, breathed life into it. This son was none other than Lord Ganesha, who emerged as a handsome and elephant-headed boy.

Ganesha was an obedient and loving child, and Parvati adored him. He became the guardian of their home, ensuring that no one entered when his mother was taking her bath or resting.

One day, Lord Shiva returned home from his meditation and was surprised to find a young boy barring his entry. Unaware of Ganesha's divine origins, Shiva became angry and, in a fit of rage, beheaded the young guardian.

Upon seeing the lifeless body of her beloved son, Parvati was devastated. She demanded that Shiva bring Ganesha back to life. To make amends, Lord Shiva replaced Ganesha's head with that of an elephant and brought him back to life.

This incident transformed Ganesha into a revered deity, known as the Lord of Beginnings and the Remover of Obstacles. He is often invoked at the start of any new venture or journey, and his benevolent presence continues to bless the lives of millions.

And that is the story of how Lord Ganesha, with his elephant head, became a beloved and widely worshiped deity in Hindu mythology.

Ganesha and the Mango Contest

One day, Lord Shiva and Goddess Parvati were sitting in their heavenly abode, Kailash, with their sons, Lord Ganesha and Lord Kartikeya. The two brothers were quite competitive and often tried to outdo each other.

On this particular day, a dispute arose about who was the wiser and more deserving of respect. To settle the argument, Lord Shiva proposed a challenge. He told them that whoever could circumambulate the universe three times and return to Kailash first would be considered the wiser of the two.

Kartikeya, full of youthful enthusiasm, quickly mounted his peacock and set off on his journey around the universe. However, Ganesha, who was known for his wisdom, took a different approach. Instead of physically circling the cosmos, he decided to circumambulate his divine parents, Lord Shiva and Goddess Parvati.

Ganesha knew that his parents represented the entire universe, and by circumambulating them, he symbolically encircled the cosmos three times. Kartikeya, meanwhile, traveled around the universe at a rapid pace.

When Kartikeya returned to Kailash after completing his journey, he was confident of his victory. However, he was surprised to find Ganesha already present. Ganesha had successfully circumambulated his parents, and his wisdom had won the day.

This story teaches us that wisdom and intelligence often surpass physical prowess, and Lord Ganesha's devotion to his parents exemplifies the importance of family and respect. Ganesha's victory in this contest also highlights his unique qualities as the deity who removes obstacles and brings wisdom to those who seek his blessings.

The Tale of Lord Ganesha
and the Broken Tusk

One day, Lord Ganesha was given the task of transcribing the epic Indian epic, the Mahabharata. He accepted this duty with great devotion and began writing it down with his quill. As he wrote, he noticed that his quill was running out of ink. Without a moment's hesitation, he decided to continue writing using his tusk.

While he was diligently transcribing the epic, Lord Ganesha's tusk broke. But he didn't stop; he continued writing with the broken tusk. His dedication to the task was unwavering.

The sage Vyasa, who was narrating the Mahabharata to Ganesha, was deeply moved by Ganesha's commitment. He praised Ganesha for his dedication and remarked that the wisdom of Ganesha would forever be associated with the Mahabharata.

Ganesha's broken tusk symbolizes sacrifice, dedication, and the willingness to overcome obstacles for a higher purpose. It's a reminder that one should not let challenges hinder the pursuit of knowledge, wisdom, and truth.

This story reflects Lord Ganesha's role as the remover of obstacles and the patron of knowledge, making him a revered deity in Hindu culture.

Lord Ganesha and the Moon

One evening, as Lord Ganesha was strolling through a forest, he noticed a beautiful full moon shining in the night sky. Ganesha was captivated by the moon's luminous beauty and couldn't take his eyes off it. He decided to have some fun and playfully mounted his mouse, his trusted vehicle, and began to chase the moon.

The moon, flustered and feeling chased by the elephant-headed deity, darted across the sky, trying to evade Ganesha's pursuit. This playful chase continued for a while, creating a celestial spectacle that caught the attention of the gods and goddesses in the heavens.

To end the fun, Lord Indra, the king of gods, decided to intervene. He hurled his thunderbolt, causing a bolt of lightning to flash across the sky and strike Lord Ganesha. The powerful bolt wounded Ganesha, and he fell to the ground, unconscious.

Seeing the consequences of his actions, Lord Indra immediately regretted his impulsive act. The gods and goddesses rushed to Ganesha's aid, and Lord Shiva, his father, was particularly distressed by the situation. To console his son, Lord Shiva revived him by placing a new head on his shoulders, an elephant head.

This incident made Lord Ganesha even more distinct and divine. He became a symbol of wisdom, intelligence, and resilience, often invoked to overcome life's challenges. The story also serves as a reminder of the importance of respecting and appreciating the beauty of the natural world without causing harm.

Lord Ganesha and the
Broken Tusk - Part II

Once, a devotee approached Lord Ganesha and asked him why he had a broken tusk. Ganesha, known for his love for his devotees, decided to share the story behind his broken tusk.

Lord Ganesha began to recount:

"Long ago, I was guarding the entrance to my mother Parvati's abode while she was taking a bath. Lord Kubera, the god of wealth, visited with a sumptuous feast as an offering to my mother. I couldn't resist the tempting aroma of the food, and my hunger got the better of me. I decided to partake in the feast.

However, my voracious appetite caused me to consume everything, leaving nothing for my mother. I was full and couldn't eat any more, but I didn't want my mother to be disappointed. So, I did the only thing I could think of. I broke off a piece of my own tusk and used it as a makeshift quill to transcribe the epic poem 'Saraswati Vandana,' which I then offered to my mother as a symbol of my love and devotion.

My mother, Parvati, was deeply moved by my sacrifice and blessed me with even more wisdom and love. And it is because of this broken tusk and my dedication to knowledge and devotion that I am known as the Lord of Beginnings and the Remover of Obstacles."

The devotee listened to Ganesha's story with awe and reverence, gaining a deeper understanding of the deity's wisdom, humility, and boundless love for his devotees.

Lord Ganesha and the Writing Competition

Once, there was a great intellectual gathering of sages, scholars, and poets in the divine realm. They were gathered to determine who among them was the most knowledgeable and eloquent. The competition was fierce, and the participants were eager to prove their wisdom.

Lord Ganesha, the deity of knowledge and wisdom, arrived at the event. His elephant head and portly appearance drew the attention of the other contestants, some of whom began to mock him. They couldn't believe that an elephant-headed deity could participate in such a competition.

To everyone's surprise, Lord Ganesha confidently stepped forward and proposed a unique challenge. He declared that he would be the subject of the competition. The participants would compete to compose verses and poetry praising his qualities and attributes. Ganesha explained that he would grant victory to the one who presented the most beautiful and truthful praise.

The competition began, and the poets and scholars struggled to find words that could capture the essence of Lord Ganesha's greatness. After much effort, they presented their compositions, which were indeed beautiful, but none truly encompassed the entirety of Ganesha's divine nature.

Finally, it was Ganesha's turn to speak. With grace and humility, he recited verses that not only praised himself but also acknowledged the talents and wisdom of the other participants. His words were filled with profound insight and touched the hearts of all present.

Lord Ganesha's poetic tribute was deemed the most extraordinary, and he was declared the winner of the competition. The other participants realized the depth of his wisdom and the greatness of his character.

This story highlights Lord Ganesha's humility, wisdom, and his role as the patron of knowledge. It reminds us that true wisdom is not just about self-praise but also recognizing the worth and talents of others.

Lord Ganesha and the
Broken Tusk - Part III

One day, a curious young boy approached Lord Ganesha and asked about the story behind his broken tusk. Ganesha, always ready to impart wisdom, shared another version of the tale:

"Long ago, as I was guarding the entrance to my mother Parvati's abode, a demon named Gajamukha, who was a devotee of Lord Shiva, approached me. He was known for his relentless determination and his deep love for Lord Shiva. Gajamukha wanted to see Lord Shiva, but I, in my role as the guardian, denied him entry because my mother was in seclusion.

The demon was undeterred and determined to meet his beloved deity. A fierce battle ensued between us. Gajamukha had incredible strength, but I was equally determined to protect my mother's privacy. In the midst of our intense struggle, I used my tusk as a weapon and struck a powerful blow to defeat the demon.

The force of the blow was so great that it broke my tusk, and Gajamukha was defeated. Seeing my determination and devotion to my mother, Lord Shiva was pleased and granted Gajamukha a place in his divine abode.

This incident not only symbolizes my dedication to my mother but also my readiness to defend her honor. It is a reminder that I will do whatever it takes to protect and serve those who are devoted to me."

The young boy listened to the story with admiration for Ganesha's unwavering commitment to his mother and his devotees, gaining a deeper understanding of the deity's courage and devotion.

Lord Ganesha and the
Mango Fruit

Once, Sage Narada, a mischievous and clever celestial sage, visited Lord Shiva and Goddess Parvati at their abode. Knowing Narada's playful nature, Parvati decided to test his wits. She presented him with a beautiful mango and suggested a contest.

Parvati said, "Narada, you are known for your knowledge and wisdom. Please take this mango and give it to the person you consider the most deserving."

Narada accepted the challenge with enthusiasm and set off on his journey. He pondered for a moment and thought, "Who could be more deserving than Lord Shiva or their sons Ganesha and Kartikeya?" But he wanted to make the contest interesting.

Narada approached Lord Shiva and presented the mango, explaining the challenge. Lord Shiva, knowing Narada's intent, agreed to participate and decided to visit Ganesha and Kartikeya to ask them to prove their worthiness.

Lord Shiva visited his two sons and explained the situation. He suggested a contest: whoever could encircle the world three times and return first would receive the mango.

Kartikeya, the younger of the two, immediately mounted his peacock and set off to circumnavigate the world. He was swift and confident in his abilities.

Ganesha, however, took a different approach. Instead of physically traveling the world, he walked around his parents three times and bowed to them, recognizing them as the entire universe.

When Kartikeya returned after completing his journey, he was triumphant. However, to his surprise, he found Ganesha already there, having encircled his parents three times.

Lord Shiva and Goddess Parvati were delighted by Ganesha's wisdom and devotion. Narada, in his mischievous challenge, had inadvertently shown the profound wisdom of Ganesha. They declared Ganesha as the most deserving and awarded him the mango.

This story teaches us about the significance of wisdom, humility, and devotion over external accomplishments. It reinforces Lord Ganesha's role as a deity of knowledge and the remover of obstacles.

Lord Ganesha and the Rat's Devotion

Lord Ganesha, the elephant-headed god, was well-known for his love of modak (sweet dumplings) and laddoos (sweet treats). One day, while he was enjoying these delicious offerings, a tiny rat scurried into the temple and approached Ganesha.

The rat, named Mushika, felt a deep sense of devotion for Lord Ganesha and wanted to show his love and dedication. Mushika offered a single laddoo to Ganesha as a token of his affection.

Ganesha, touched by the rat's sincere offering, accepted the laddoo with gratitude. He also lovingly patted Mushika on the head to bless him.

This simple act of devotion deeply moved Lord Ganesha, and he declared that from that day forward, Mushika would be his vehicle. The rat, now transformed into a giant rat, became Ganesha's trusted mount.

Mushika, despite his small size, carried Lord Ganesha with great pride and devotion. He became a symbol of how even the smallest creatures can receive the blessings of the divine through their unwavering devotion.

This story highlights Lord Ganesha's compassion and the importance of devotion in one's relationship with the divine. It also explains why Ganesha is often depicted with Mushika (the rat) as his vehicle.

Lord Ganesha and the Broken Tusk - Part IV

In another episode of Lord Ganesha's life, he embarked on a journey to help a poor and humble sculptor.

One day, a sculptor named Gana lived in a small village. He was known for his devotion to Lord Shiva and longed to create an idol of the deity for his local temple. Gana was a talented artist but could not find a suitable material to craft the idol. He was also very poor and could not afford expensive sculpting tools.

Desperate to fulfill his dream, Gana decided to fashion an idol from clay he gathered from the riverbed. With utmost devotion, he began crafting the image of Lord Shiva. However, his rudimentary tools were not suitable for the detailed work he wished to achieve.

Lord Ganesha, known for his love for his devotees, appeared before Gana in a dream. He offered to help the sculptor and instructed him to use the broken tusk of an elephant he would find by the riverbank. Gana followed the divine guidance and found the broken tusk as instructed.

With Lord Ganesha's tusk, Gana was able to carve a beautiful and intricate idol of Lord Shiva. The idol was not only praised for its exquisite craftsmanship but also for the deep devotion that went into creating it.

The villagers were amazed by Gana's creation and his devotion. The idol became the centerpiece of the temple, and Gana's name became synonymous with artistry and devotion in the village.

This story reflects Lord Ganesha's role as the patron of the arts and his compassion for those who are devoted to him. It also symbolizes the idea that even the most humble and unlikely materials can be transformed into something divine through unwavering devotion.

Lord Ganesha and the
Lost Scriptures

In ancient times, a great sage named Vyasa had composed a set of sacred scriptures known as the "Mahabharata," which contained the knowledge of the ages. These scriptures were written on palm leaves and were immensely precious.

Vyasa was worried that this invaluable knowledge might be lost to future generations because the scriptures were difficult to understand and interpret. He prayed to Lord Brahma for guidance.

Lord Brahma, the creator of the universe, instructed Vyasa to seek the help of Lord Ganesha in transcribing the scriptures. Vyasa approached Ganesha and explained his predicament. Ganesha, known for his wisdom, agreed to help.

The task was enormous, and Ganesha began to write the Mahabharata as Vyasa dictated it. However, Ganesha set a unique condition for his assistance. He would write only if Vyasa continued narrating the epic without interruption. Vyasa, in turn, imposed a condition that Ganesha should understand the verses completely before writing them down.

As the process continued, Vyasa realized that he needed breaks to compose new verses. He used these breaks to recite complex verses to give himself time to think. Ganesha, who was writing quickly to keep up, broke off his own tusk to use as a quill, so as not to interrupt the flow of the narration.

The completion of this monumental task resulted in the Mahabharata, one of the most significant and extensive epics in Hindu literature. Ganesha's sacrifice of his tusk for the sake of knowledge is a symbol of his selflessness and his commitment to preserving wisdom for future generations.

This story highlights Lord Ganesha's role as the deity of knowledge and underscores the importance of understanding and preserving sacred texts and wisdom.

Lord Ganesha and the
Mango Orchard

Once, there was a devout farmer named Ramesh who owned a mango orchard. His mangoes were renowned for their sweetness and flavor. Every year, he would offer the first mango of the season to Lord Ganesha as a mark of his deep faith and gratitude.

One year, as the mango season approached, Ramesh noticed that one of his mangoes was growing unusually large and beautiful. He believed it to be the finest mango he had ever seen and decided that this mango would be the special offering to Lord Ganesha.

As the day of the offering arrived, Ramesh carefully plucked the exquisite mango, wrapped it in silk, and placed it on his offering plate. He headed to the temple with a heart full of devotion.

Upon reaching the temple, he placed the mango at the feet of Lord Ganesha and offered his prayers. As he was about to leave, a beggar outside the temple asked for food. Ramesh, known for his generosity, decided to share the mango with the beggar.

When he returned to the temple, he was shocked to find that the exquisite mango had miraculously reappeared on the offering plate. This happened again when he shared it with another beggar. Ramesh realized that Lord Ganesha was testing his devotion and selflessness.

Understanding the divine message, Ramesh returned home, picked the mango once more, and decided to offer half to the beggars and the other half to Lord Ganesha. This time, when he left the temple, the mango did not reappear.

Ramesh felt a deep sense of fulfillment and knew that his devotion and selflessness had been accepted by Lord Ganesha.

This story emphasizes the importance of selflessness and devotion and shows how Lord Ganesha tests and rewards the sincerity of his devotees.

Lord Ganesha and the Elephant Companion

Once, in a distant village, a poor farmer named Raj was plowing his fields with his faithful elephant companion, Gaja. Gaja was a magnificent and gentle elephant, loved by the entire village. Raj and Gaja had a deep bond, and they worked together tirelessly.

One day, as they were plowing the fields, a sudden storm approached. Lightning struck, and a massive tree fell towards Raj. Without hesitation, Gaja shielded his beloved owner with his own body, taking the full force of the falling tree.

Tragically, Gaja lost his life protecting Raj. The villagers were heartbroken, and Raj was overcome with grief. He realized that Gaja's sacrifice was a supreme act of love and devotion.

In his grief, Raj carved an image of Lord Ganesha to honor the elephant's sacrifice. He prayed to Ganesha, asking for his blessings and protection for his family and the entire village. Ganesha, known as the remover of obstacles, was deeply moved by the story of Gaja's sacrifice and appeared before Raj.

Lord Ganesha blessed Raj and his village, promising to protect them from all adversity. The elephant-headed deity became the guardian of the village, and the villagers erected a temple in his honor.

This story illustrates the compassion of Lord Ganesha and the importance of selfless devotion, as exemplified by the faithful elephant Gaja. It also underscores Ganesha's role as a protector and guardian of those who seek his divine intervention.

Lord Ganesha and the
Singing Mouse

In a peaceful village, there lived a devout musician named Ravi who was known for his enchanting flute melodies. He was also a devoted worshipper of Lord Ganesha. Each morning, he would offer his prayers to Ganesha and play his flute in devotion.

One day, as Ravi was playing his flute by the riverside, a tiny mouse, named Surila, approached him. Surila was drawn to the mesmerizing music and began to dance to the tunes of Ravi's flute. This sight was enchanting, and Ravi was delighted to see the little mouse enjoying his melodies.

Afterward, Surila approached Ravi and whispered, "Dear musician, your music has touched my heart. If you permit me, I would love to stay with you and listen to your melodies every day."

Ravi was moved by Surila's words and agreed to let the mouse stay in his humble abode. Surila became a regular companion to Ravi, and their friendship deepened over time. Surila would sit by Ravi's side, listening to his music and occasionally dancing to the tunes.

One day, while Ravi was practicing, a venomous snake slithered into their home. Surila, determined to protect her dear friend, started to sing aloud and danced vigorously to distract the snake. Ravi, realizing the danger, swiftly took action and managed to shoo the snake away.

Ravi and Surila were both unharmed, but Surila's small body was exhausted from her efforts. She fell into Ravi's lap and passed away.

Ravi, in his grief, couldn't bear the loss of his beloved friend. He prayed to Lord Ganesha, seeking his divine intervention. Ganesha, moved by Ravi's devotion and the bravery of the singing mouse, granted Surila a new life. She came back to life, and Ravi's joy knew no bounds.

The people in the village came to know of this miraculous event and realized the depth of Lord Ganesha's compassion. They began to worship Ganesha with even greater devotion, understanding that the deity valued even the smallest acts of love and bravery.

This story illustrates the compassion of Lord Ganesha and the importance of devotion and gratitude. It also highlights that Ganesha values not only grand gestures but also the small, heartfelt acts of love and courage.

Lord Ganesha and the
Lost Necklace

In a bustling marketplace, there lived a poor woman named Leela. She had a simple but precious necklace that was passed down to her by her ancestors. It was a symbol of her family's heritage and a cherished possession.

One day, while shopping for vegetables in the market, Leela's necklace accidentally slipped off her neck and fell into a vendor's basket. She realized her loss only when she returned home. Distraught, she rushed back to the market, searching for her precious necklace.

Leela approached the vendor and explained her situation, but the vendor denied having seen the necklace, insisting that his basket contained only vegetables. The poor woman was heartbroken, as the necklace held immense sentimental value for her.

Desperate, Leela visited a nearby temple and prayed fervently to Lord Ganesha, the remover of obstacles. She asked for his help in finding her lost necklace. Ganesha, known for his compassionate nature, appeared before Leela.

He asked Leela to return to the marketplace and speak to the vendor once more. Ganesha advised her to mention that she had prayed to Lord Ganesha for help in finding the necklace.

Leela followed Ganesha's guidance and returned to the market. This time, when she spoke to the vendor and mentioned her prayer to Ganesha, the vendor's demeanor changed. He felt a sense of guilt and confessed to having found the necklace in his basket but was unsure how to return it.

Leela's necklace was returned to her, and she was overcome with gratitude to Lord Ganesha for his divine intervention.

This story illustrates Lord Ganesha's role as the remover of obstacles and how devotion and seeking his assistance can help overcome challenges and recover lost possessions. It also emphasizes the importance of honesty and compassion in resolving difficult situations.

Lord Ganesha and the
Fruit Vendor

In a bustling marketplace, there was a kind-hearted fruit vendor named Ramu. He was known for his honesty and generosity. Each day, he would offer a portion of his fruits to Lord Ganesha, whom he had deep devotion for.

One hot summer's day, a poor beggar approached Ramu's fruit cart, his face parched and weary. He asked Ramu for a piece of fruit or a sip of water. Ramu, true to his nature, offered the beggar a juicy mango and some cool water.

As the beggar savored the delicious mango, he noticed a small idol of Lord Ganesha near the cart and asked Ramu about it. Ramu explained his deep reverence for Ganesha and how he offered a portion of his daily earnings to the deity.

The beggar, who was actually Lord Ganesha in disguise, was moved by Ramu's kindness and devotion. To test Ramu further, he said, "If you offer a portion of your earnings to Ganesha, then I wish to give you something in return. I have this magical mango that will bring you immense wealth and prosperity. Will you accept it?"

Ramu, being an honest and devout man, replied, "Thank you, but I am content with what I have. Lord Ganesha has always provided for me, and I don't seek wealth or magical mangoes. I am happy with my simple life and helping those in need."

At that moment, the beggar revealed his true form as Lord Ganesha. He appeared before Ramu, showering him with blessings and revealing his divine nature. Ganesha commended Ramu for his sincerity and devotion.

From that day on, Ramu's fruit cart became even more prosperous, and he continued to offer a portion of his earnings to Lord Ganesha. His story of unwavering faith and devotion inspired many in the village to follow in his footsteps.

This story exemplifies Lord Ganesha's appreciation for sincere devotion and the rewards it can bring. It also emphasizes the importance of humility and contentment in the face of material temptations.

Lord Ganesha and the Lost Ring

In a small village, there lived a humble washerwoman named Lata. She had a simple gold ring that she cherished dearly; it was a gift from her late mother. Lata considered it her most precious possession.

One sunny morning, as she was washing clothes by the river, she noticed that her beloved ring had slipped off her finger and fallen into the flowing water. Panicked, she searched the riverbank in vain, but the ring was nowhere to be found.

Heartbroken and in tears, Lata returned home and prayed to Lord Ganesha, asking for his help in recovering her lost ring. She promised to offer a special prayer to Ganesha at the village temple if her ring was returned to her.

Ganesha, known for his compassion, heard Lata's sincere plea. He took the form of a young boy and appeared before her. The boy asked Lata about her distress, and she explained her situation, telling him about the lost ring and her promise to Ganesha.

The young boy reassured Lata and told her to return to the riverbank the next morning. He promised to help her find the lost ring.

The next day, as the sun rose, Lata returned to the riverbank, accompanied by the young boy. She watched in astonishment as the boy recited a prayer to Lord Ganesha and gently touched the water. To her amazement, the river calmed, and her lost ring emerged from the depths, gleaming in the morning light.

Lata was overjoyed and realized that the young boy was a manifestation of Lord Ganesha himself. She thanked the deity for his divine intervention and fulfilled her promise by offering a special prayer at the village temple.

The villagers were astounded by the miracle and gained a renewed appreciation for the power of devotion to Lord Ganesha. This story highlights Ganesha's compassion and willingness to help his devotees, even in the most challenging of situations. It also underscores the importance of keeping one's promises and showing gratitude for divine blessings.

Lord Ganesha and the Fisherwoman's Offering

In a quaint fishing village, there lived a devoted fisherwoman named Meera. Each day, she would venture out to the sea, cast her nets, and bring back fresh catches to feed her family. Meera also had a deep reverence for Lord Ganesha, whom she considered her divine protector on the treacherous waters.

One stormy day, while she was out at sea, a massive wave capsized her boat. Meera clung to a piece of driftwood, struggling to stay afloat. As the sea raged around her, she prayed fervently to Lord Ganesha for safety and guidance.

Miraculously, her prayer was answered. A giant turtle appeared in the water, and Meera managed to climb onto its back. The turtle carried her safely to the shore. She thanked the turtle and made her way home, still in awe of the divine intervention.

Meera, out of profound gratitude, decided to honor Lord Ganesha for saving her life. She offered a beautiful conch shell, a symbol of the sea, to a small shrine dedicated to Ganesha in the village.

One evening, as she was offering the conch shell, she noticed that the shrine had become brighter and more radiant. To her astonishment, the conch shell she had offered now contained a beautiful pearl, gleaming with a divine glow.

Meera realized that Lord Ganesha had accepted her humble offering and blessed her with the precious pearl as a token of his gratitude for her unwavering devotion.

The story of Meera's miraculous rescue and the divine gift of the pearl became well-known in the village. It served as a testament to the power of faith and the blessings that Lord Ganesha bestows on those who seek his protection and guidance.

This story illustrates Ganesha's role as the protector and guardian of those who face challenges, as well as the profound impact of genuine devotion and gratitude.

Lord Ganesha and the Caring Potter

In a village, there lived a skilled potter named Raman. He was not only known for his craftsmanship but also for his caring and humble nature. Raman had a small idol of Lord Ganesha in his workshop, and every morning, he would offer a handful of freshly made clay modaks (sweet dumplings) to Ganesha as a token of his devotion.

One monsoon, a severe storm ravaged the village, leaving many people homeless and in dire need of shelter. Raman, with a compassionate heart, opened his home to those who had lost their houses. He provided them with food, shelter, and a safe haven.

As days turned into weeks, Raman's own financial situation began to suffer, but he did not waver in his commitment to helping those in need. He continued to care for the displaced villagers, despite the hardships he faced.

One evening, as Raman prepared to offer his usual handful of modaks to Lord Ganesha, he realized he had run out of clay to make them. Desperate and worried, he prayed to Ganesha, explaining his predicament and asking for guidance.

That night, Raman had a dream in which Lord Ganesha appeared before him. The deity smiled and said, "Your kindness and compassion have already offered the sweetest modak, dear Raman. I am immensely pleased with your selfless actions."

Raman woke up with a sense of reassurance and continued to care for the villagers. To his astonishment, he found a large sack of clay outside his workshop the next morning. With that clay, he was able to make more modaks and offer them to Lord Ganesha.

The villagers eventually found new homes, and Raman's own hardships began to ease. He believed that it was Lord Ganesha's blessings and the divine acknowledgment of his selflessness that had brought relief to his life.

This story exemplifies Lord Ganesha's appreciation for acts of kindness and selflessness, even when faced with personal challenges. It underscores the idea that genuine compassion and devotion can bring divine blessings and fulfillment.

Lord Ganesha and the Farmer's Bountiful Harvest

In a remote village, there lived a humble farmer named Ramesh. Ramesh was known for his unwavering devotion to Lord Ganesha, and he would often offer a portion of his harvest to the deity in a small shrine near his farm.

One year, due to unfavorable weather conditions, the entire village faced a severe drought, and the crops began to wither. The villagers were worried about their livelihoods and the well-being of their families.

Ramesh, however, remained steadfast in his devotion. He continued to tend to his fields and offered his prayers to Lord Ganesha, asking for help during this difficult time.

One night, in a vivid dream, Lord Ganesha appeared before Ramesh. The deity smiled and told him, "Ramesh, your devotion has touched my heart. You have remained steadfast in your faith even in the face of adversity. As a token of my blessings, go to your fields tomorrow and harvest the crop."

Ramesh woke up with a renewed sense of hope and followed Lord Ganesha's instructions. When he reached his fields, he was astounded to find an abundant harvest of healthy crops, unlike anything he had ever seen. The entire village marveled at the miraculous turn of events.

Ramesh shared his experience and the bountiful harvest with the villagers. They all realized that it was the result of Ramesh's unwavering faith and Lord Ganesha's blessings.

The village celebrated the harvest, and Ramesh continued to offer his gratitude to Lord Ganesha, reaffirming his deep devotion. The story of Ramesh's miracle harvest became well-known in the region, serving as a reminder of the power of faith and the divine intervention of Lord Ganesha in times of need.

This story illustrates Ganesha's role as the remover of obstacles and the provider of blessings during challenging times. It also emphasizes the significance of unwavering faith and devotion.

Lord Ganesha and the
Generous Potter

In a quiet village, there lived a skilled potter named Govind. He was not just known for his craftsmanship but also for his boundless generosity. Every year, during the festival dedicated to Lord Ganesha, Govind would create a beautifully crafted idol of the deity and offer it in the village temple.

One year, the festival approached, and Govind was eager to create a new idol that would be even more magnificent than before. However, he faced a dilemma as he was short of the finest clay to craft the idol.

Undeterred, Govind began shaping the idol with the clay he had. He put all his love and devotion into the creation, hoping that Lord Ganesha would understand his situation.

As Govind finished the idol and placed it in the temple, a miracle occurred. The idol transformed into a radiant, golden image of Lord Ganesha, with a divine aura that filled the temple. The villagers were astounded by the divine intervention.

It was clear that Lord Ganesha had not only accepted Govind's humble offering but also bestowed his blessings upon the generous potter. The entire village celebrated the miraculous event and recognized Govind's unwavering devotion and selflessness.

This story highlights the power of devotion and the compassion of Lord Ganesha, as well as the belief that sincere offerings, regardless of their material value, are cherished by the divine.

Lord Ganesha and the Farmer's Enchanted Garden

In a rural village, there lived a diligent farmer named Vikram. He toiled tirelessly to cultivate his land and support his family. Vikram had a small garden near his home, where he grew a variety of fruits and vegetables to sustain his household.

One year, a severe drought struck the region, and Vikram's garden began to wither. Despite his best efforts, the lack of water and scorching heat took a toll on his precious crops. Desperate to save his garden, Vikram prayed to Lord Ganesha, seeking divine assistance.

In his prayer, Vikram made a heartfelt promise that if Lord Ganesha helped revive his garden, he would share the bountiful harvest with those in need and provide free meals to the hungry in his village.

Touched by Vikram's sincerity and his commitment to helping others, Lord Ganesha appeared in the garden. He blessed the land and, with a wave of his trunk, transformed the garden into a lush, vibrant oasis. The crops grew abundantly, despite the ongoing drought.

True to his promise, Vikram kept his word. He shared the harvest from his enchanted garden with the less fortunate in his village and began providing daily meals to the hungry. The news of Vikram's generosity and the miraculous transformation of his garden spread far and wide.

Vikram's garden not only brought prosperity to his family but also provided for the entire community. It became a symbol of hope, kindness, and the power of unwavering devotion to Lord Ganesha.

This story illustrates the compassion of Lord Ganesha and the profound impact of heartfelt promises and acts of kindness. It emphasizes the idea that faith and dedication to helping others can lead to blessings and miracles.

Lord Ganesha and the Loyal Hermit

In a remote forest, there resided a devoted hermit named Narayan. He had spent his entire life in solitude, meditating and seeking spiritual enlightenment. Narayan's only companion was a loyal elephant named Parvani, who had been with him since her calfhood.

The bond between Narayan and Parvani was profound, and they shared a deep spiritual connection. Every day, Narayan would meditate under the shade of a large banyan tree, and Parvani would stand guard, ensuring his safety.

One day, while Narayan was deep in meditation, a group of hunters entered the forest, hoping to capture and tame Parvani for the grandeur of the royal court. The hunters used tricks and deceit to separate Parvani from Narayan and began their journey back with her.

Narayan, upon awakening from his meditation and realizing what had transpired, was distraught. He prayed fervently to Lord Ganesha for assistance in reuniting with his beloved companion.

Moved by Narayan's devotion, Lord Ganesha appeared before him in the form of a young boy. Ganesha assured Narayan that he would help him recover Parvani and asked him to have faith.

With Ganesha's guidance, Narayan set out on a journey to find Parvani. He encountered various challenges, faced adversity, and displayed unwavering determination. Along the way, he received help from unexpected sources, such as friendly animals and kind-hearted villagers who guided him in the right direction.

After a long and arduous journey, Narayan finally reached the royal court, where Parvani was being held. He explained the depth of his bond with the elephant and the lessons they had learned together in the forest.

Touched by Narayan's story, the king and the royal court decided to release Parvani and return her to her rightful place with Narayan. The reunited hermit and elephant returned to their forest home.

Narayan knew that it was Lord Ganesha's divine intervention and guidance that had led him to Parvani and helped them overcome the challenges they faced. He continued his spiritual practices under the banyan tree, with Parvani standing by his side.

This story exemplifies the compassionate and guiding nature of Lord Ganesha and underscores the importance of faith, determination, and the strength of the human-animal bond.

Lord Ganesha and the
Weaver's Miracle

In a small weaving village, there lived a skilled weaver named Meena. She was known for her intricate and beautiful silk sarees, which were highly sought after in the region. Meena was not only a talented weaver but also a devout devotee of Lord Ganesha.

One year, as the festival dedicated to Lord Ganesha approached, Meena decided to create a special silk saree as an offering to the deity. She used the finest silk threads, weaving it with great care and dedication, creating an exquisite piece of art that depicted the life of Lord Ganesha.

However, when the time came to complete the saree, Meena realized that she had run out of the silk thread. She was heartbroken and worried that she wouldn't be able to finish her offering in time for the festival.

With tears in her eyes, Meena prayed to Lord Ganesha, asking for his guidance and assistance. She promised to continue creating beautiful silk sarees in his honor if he helped her complete the one at hand.

Lord Ganesha, moved by Meena's sincerity, decided to help her. That night, in a dream, he showed her the way to a hidden silkworm cocoon deep in the forest, promising that it contained the perfect thread for her saree.

Meena followed Ganesha's guidance and ventured into the forest. She found the hidden silkworm cocoon and carefully collected the silk thread. With this special thread, she completed the saree, which was a masterpiece of craftsmanship.

The saree was presented to Lord Ganesha during the festival, and it was admired by all who saw it. Meena continued to create beautiful silk sarees in Ganesha's honor, and her skills as a weaver became renowned throughout the land.

This story illustrates Ganesha's role as a guide and helper in times of need, as well as the importance of heartfelt offerings and promises. It also underscores the idea that devotion and dedication are rewarded by divine blessings.

Lord Ganesha and the
Artist's Inspiration

In a bustling city, there lived a struggling artist named Maya. She was passionate about her craft and would create beautiful paintings that reflected the beauty of the world. However, her artistic inspiration had faded, and she was going through a creative block.

Maya had a small shrine dedicated to Lord Ganesha in her studio. One day, she decided to offer a heartfelt prayer, seeking inspiration to bring her art back to life. She promised to use her talents to spread joy and positivity through her paintings.

Touched by Maya's sincerity, Lord Ganesha appeared in a dream that night. He handed her a paintbrush and encouraged her to create art from the heart, without any reservations or doubts. Ganesha's message was clear: to embrace her unique perspective and not be afraid to express herself.

Inspired by the divine encounter, Maya woke up with a newfound sense of purpose. She began painting with a renewed vigor, pouring her emotions and creativity into her artwork. Her paintings transformed, filled with vibrant colors, intricate details, and a sense of joy.

Maya's work garnered the attention of art enthusiasts and collectors, and her reputation as an artist grew. She organized exhibitions and used her art to inspire and uplift others. Her paintings became a source of happiness and hope for many.

The story of Maya's transformation and the inspiration she received from Lord Ganesha spread far and wide, serving as a reminder of the creative spark that can be ignited through faith and devotion. It also emphasizes the importance of pursuing one's passions with dedication and authenticity.

Lord Ganesha and the
Compassionate Healer

In a bustling town, there lived a skilled healer named Dr. Aman. He was renowned for his knowledge of herbal remedies and his unwavering commitment to helping those in need. Dr. Aman had a small clinic where he treated patients from all walks of life, providing his services free of charge to those who couldn't afford medical care.

One day, Dr. Aman encountered a patient named Priya, a young girl who was suffering from a rare and severe illness. Despite his best efforts, Dr. Aman couldn't find a cure for her condition. Priya's family was devastated, and the girl's health continued to deteriorate.

In his despair, Dr. Aman turned to Lord Ganesha, praying for guidance and a solution to save Priya. He promised to dedicate his life to serving the sick and needy if Ganesha would help him find a cure.

Touched by Dr. Aman's compassion and devotion, Lord Ganesha appeared before him. He provided Dr. Aman with a unique herb that could heal Priya's rare illness. Ganesha instructed Dr. Aman on how to prepare the remedy and administer it to the young girl.

Dr. Aman followed Ganesha's guidance, and within a few weeks, Priya's health began to improve. She made a full recovery, and her family was filled with gratitude for Dr. Aman's expertise and care.

True to his promise, Dr. Aman dedicated his life to serving the sick and needy, offering free medical care to those who couldn't afford it. His clinic became a place of hope and healing, and his reputation as a compassionate healer grew.

The story of Dr. Aman's miraculous cure and the impact of his compassionate service spread throughout the town, reminding people of the power of faith, devotion, and the role of Lord Ganesha in providing guidance and solutions during challenging times.

This story highlights Ganesha's role as a guide and provider of solutions, as well as the significance of compassion and selfless service to those in need.

Lord Ganesha and the Musician's Harmonious Concert

In a lively town, there lived a gifted musician named Rohit. He was not only a master of the flute but also a devoted worshipper of Lord Ganesha. Rohit would start each day with a musical tribute to the deity, playing his flute in praise and devotion.

One year, a grand music festival was announced in the town, and Rohit was excited to participate. He decided to compose a new piece that would blend classical and contemporary music to create a unique symphony.

As he composed the piece, Rohit encountered creative blocks, unable to find the perfect blend of traditional and modern melodies. He turned to Lord Ganesha for guidance, promising to dedicate the performance to the deity if he received divine inspiration.

One night, Lord Ganesha appeared to Rohit in a dream. He played a hauntingly beautiful melody on his own divine flute and encouraged Rohit to infuse his composition with the same spirit. Ganesha's music was both traditional and modern, a harmonious blend of the old and the new.

Inspired by the dream, Rohit woke up and began to play the melody he had heard. With Ganesha's guidance, he composed a mesmerizing piece that showcased the perfect fusion of classical and contemporary music.

During the music festival, Rohit's performance left the audience spellbound. His composition received accolades for its innovation and beauty, and it brought a sense of unity and harmony to the town.

Rohit fulfilled his promise to dedicate the performance to Lord Ganesha, recognizing the deity's role as his divine muse. The story of the musician's divine inspiration became a testament to the power of faith and the creative guidance that Ganesha can provide.

This story emphasizes Ganesha's role as a source of inspiration and creativity, as well as the importance of dedication to one's craft and faith in the face of challenges.

Lord Ganesha and the
Noble Teacher

In a peaceful village, there lived a dedicated teacher named Suresh. He was known for his wisdom and his commitment to providing quality education to the children of the village, especially to those who could not afford schooling.

One year, the village faced a severe shortage of educational materials, and Suresh's school was in dire need of books, pens, and paper. He reached out to various sources but couldn't gather the necessary resources to continue teaching.

In his time of need, Suresh turned to Lord Ganesha, praying for guidance and assistance. He promised to teach the children with the same dedication, even if he had to do so without the required materials. Suresh sought Ganesha's blessings to overcome the obstacles he faced.

Touched by Suresh's sincerity and commitment to educating the children, Lord Ganesha appeared in a dream. He instructed Suresh to go to a specific location in the forest, where he would find a tree with leaves that could be used as paper and ink that could be extracted from a particular plant.

The next day, Suresh followed Ganesha's guidance and collected the leaves and ink as instructed. He used them to create makeshift books and writing materials for his students.

As Suresh resumed his teaching, he found that the materials provided by Ganesha were not only sufficient but also unique in their texture, making learning a more engaging and memorable experience for the children.

Word of Suresh's dedication and the miraculous appearance of educational materials spread throughout the village. People began to donate additional resources to support his noble cause.

The story of the noble teacher's unwavering commitment to education and the divine intervention of Lord Ganesha became an inspiration to the entire village. It highlighted the importance of dedication to education and the belief that challenges can be overcome through faith and devotion.

This story underscores Ganesha's role as a guide and provider of solutions, as well as the significance of education and the impact it can have on a community.

Lord Ganesha and the
Caring Innkeeper

In a bustling crossroads town, there was an inn run by a compassionate innkeeper named Anil. He was known for his warm hospitality and his dedication to ensuring that travelers and pilgrims had a comfortable place to rest.

One year, a massive flood ravaged the region, displacing many villagers and travelers. Anil's inn became a refuge for those who had lost their homes. He provided shelter, food, and comfort to all, regardless of their ability to pay.

Despite his generosity, Anil's resources were stretched to the limit. The inn's supplies were running low, and he didn't have enough provisions to sustain the growing number of people seeking refuge.

Anil turned to Lord Ganesha in his time of need, praying for help and guidance. He promised to continue providing a safe haven to those in distress, even if it meant personal sacrifice.

Lord Ganesha, moved by Anil's selflessness, appeared before him in the form of a weary traveler. Ganesha explained that he had faced a long and difficult journey and was in need of a place to rest. Anil, without realizing the traveler's true identity, welcomed him into the inn.

As the night passed, the traveler revealed his true form as Lord Ganesha and thanked Anil for his hospitality. He blessed the innkeeper, telling him to look in the storeroom of the inn.

In the storeroom, Anil discovered that it was miraculously filled with an abundance of supplies, enough to sustain his inn and the villagers who sought refuge. The floodwaters began to recede, and those who had taken shelter at Anil's inn were able to rebuild their lives.

Anil's selfless dedication to helping those in need, along with Lord Ganesha's divine intervention, became a symbol of compassion and generosity. The story emphasized the belief that acts of kindness and hospitality are never in vain and can lead to unexpected blessings.

This story highlights Ganesha's role as a provider and protector in times of crisis, as well as the significance of selfless acts of kindness and hospitality.

Lord Ganesha and the
Honest Trader

In a bustling marketplace, there was a merchant named Rajiv known for his honesty and integrity. He traded various goods, from spices to textiles, and he was respected by both customers and fellow traders.

One year, as Rajiv's business grew, he was offered a significant trade deal that would bring immense profit. However, he realized that the deal was not entirely honest and involved deceitful practices that would harm other traders in the market.

Rajiv, unwavering in his commitment to fairness, declined the offer, despite the financial gain it would have brought him. He believed in conducting his business with integrity and treating others with respect.

As a result, many traders, both new and experienced, began to look up to Rajiv as a model of honesty and ethical conduct in the marketplace. His reputation grew, and his business thrived as customers sought his goods because of his trustworthy reputation.

One day, as he continued his devotion to Lord Ganesha, Rajiv prayed for the guidance to maintain his honesty and integrity in the face of tempting offers. He promised to use his success to support charitable causes in the community.

Touched by Rajiv's unwavering commitment to honesty and fairness, Lord Ganesha appeared before him. He blessed the trader, recognizing his dedication to ethical practices and his willingness to put the welfare of others before personal gain.

With Ganesha's blessings, Rajiv's business prospered, and he used his success to support local charities and initiatives that improved the lives of those in need. His example inspired many other traders in the marketplace to prioritize honesty and fairness in their dealings.

This story underlines the importance of honesty, integrity, and ethical conduct in business, as well as the role of Lord Ganesha in guiding those who seek to do what is right. It also emphasizes the significance of using one's success for the betterment of the community.

Lord Ganesha and the Determined Farmer

In a remote farming village, there lived a determined farmer named Ramu. He was known for his unwavering dedication to tilling the land and providing sustenance for the community. However, for several years, the region faced a persistent drought that threatened the crops and the livelihood of the villagers.

Ramu refused to give in to despair. He continued to sow his seeds, tend to his fields, and offer his daily prayers to Lord Ganesha for rain and a bountiful harvest.

One day, as Ramu was working in the fields, he noticed a small, green shoot emerging from the parched soil. Surprisingly, it was a sign of life in the otherwise barren land. Over the following days, more shoots appeared, and the villagers marveled at the miraculous growth.

As the days passed, the small green shoots grew into sturdy, drought-resistant crops that thrived despite the ongoing lack of rain. Ramu's fields became a beacon of hope and an inspiration to the entire village.

The villagers believed that Lord Ganesha had intervened, providing a solution to their drought-stricken land. Ramu's unwavering faith and determination to cultivate the land, even in the face of adversity, had led to the miracle.

Ramu's success in the midst of drought became a symbol of resilience and the belief that perseverance, combined with devotion, could lead to extraordinary outcomes. It also highlighted Lord Ganesha's role as the provider of blessings and solutions during challenging times. 56

This story emphasizes the importance of determination, faith, and the resilience of the human spirit, as well as the divine intervention of Lord Ganesha in times of need.

Lord Ganesha and the
Curious Artist

In a picturesque village, there lived a curious artist named Devi. She was known for her inquisitive nature and her desire to explore and create art inspired by the wonders of the world. Devi's art was a reflection of her deep appreciation for the beauty of nature.

One year, a total solar eclipse was scheduled to occur, a rare celestial event that captured the imagination of the entire village. Devi was determined to create a painting that would capture the essence of this extraordinary event and share its wonder with the world.

As she prepared to create her masterpiece, Devi faced a challenge. She lacked the resources to safely observe the eclipse without endangering her eyesight. She was torn between her desire to witness the eclipse and her commitment to her art.

Devi turned to Lord Ganesha for guidance, praying for a solution to her dilemma. She promised to use her art to inspire others and share the beauty of the world with those who couldn't experience it firsthand.

Touched by Devi's devotion and her dedication to her art, Lord Ganesha provided her with a vision in a dream. He showed her a safe way to observe the eclipse, using a pinhole projector, which would protect her eyes while allowing her to witness the celestial spectacle.

With Ganesha's guidance, Devi created her art by observing the eclipse safely. Her painting captured the magnificence of the celestial event, and it served as a source of inspiration for the entire village, making them appreciate the beauty of the world in a new way.

Devi fulfilled her promise by using her art to share the wonder of the eclipse with others, educating them about the pinhole projector technique to observe such events safely.

This story emphasizes the value of curiosity, creativity, and the role of art in inspiring others. It also underscores the idea that with devotion and guidance, challenges can be overcome to create something beautiful and meaningful.

Lord Ganesha and the Humble Street Vendor

In a bustling city, there lived a humble street vendor named Manoj. He earned his living by selling fragrant jasmine garlands to devotees who visited the local temples. Manoj was known for his cheerful disposition and the devotion he poured into creating the most exquisite garlands.

One year, the city was preparing for a grand festival dedicated to Lord Ganesha, and thousands of devotees would gather to offer prayers and garlands at the temple. Manoj was excited to provide his fragrant creations for the occasion.

As the festival approached, Manoj faced a challenge. His supply of jasmine flowers had dwindled, and he couldn't procure more due to a sudden shortage in the market. He worried that he would not have enough garlands to meet the demand of the festival.

With a heavy heart, Manoj prayed to Lord Ganesha, asking for assistance to ensure that he could provide beautiful garlands for the devotees during the festival. He promised to make an extra effort to spread joy and positivity through his fragrant creations.

Touched by Manoj's sincerity and devotion, Lord Ganesha appeared in the form of a young flower seller. He handed Manoj a small bag of magical jasmine seeds and encouraged him to plant them.

Manoj followed Ganesha's guidance and planted the magical seeds. To his astonishment, the jasmine plants grew rapidly and produced an abundance of the most fragrant and beautiful flowers he had ever seen.

With the help of these magical jasmine flowers, Manoj was able to create the most exquisite garlands for the Ganesha festival. The garlands brought joy and comfort to the devotees who visited the temple, and they were considered the most beautiful offerings.

Manoj's devotion and the miraculous growth of the jasmine plants became a symbol of faith and the unexpected ways in which the divine can provide solutions during challenging times.

This story highlights the importance of devotion, faith, and the belief that divine help can arrive in surprising and magical ways, as well as the significance of spreading joy and positivity to others.

Lord Ganesha and the Caring Fisherwoman

In a coastal fishing village, there lived a kind-hearted fisherwoman named Lila. She was known for her generosity and her willingness to help those in need. Lila earned her living by fishing in the sea, providing sustenance for her family and the villagers.

One year, the village faced a severe food shortage due to a series of storms that disrupted the fishing season. Families were struggling to put food on the table, and many went to bed hungry.

Lila, despite her own challenges, couldn't bear to see her fellow villagers suffer. She decided to share her meager catch with those who had nothing. Every day, she distributed fish to the hungry families, ensuring that they had a meal.

As the food shortage continued, Lila prayed to Lord Ganesha for guidance and assistance. She promised to continue helping those in need, even if it meant personal sacrifice. Lila sought Ganesha's blessings to find a way to bring abundance to the sea.

Touched by Lila's selflessness and dedication to helping others, Lord Ganesha appeared before her in the form of a fisherman. He gave her a specific location in the sea, telling her that she would find an abundance of fish in that spot.

Lila followed Ganesha's guidance and sailed to the location he had mentioned. To her amazement, the sea was teeming with fish, more than she had ever seen before. She returned with a bountiful catch, providing sustenance not only for her family but also for the entire village.

Lila continued to distribute fish to those in need, and her actions inspired others in the village to help one another during difficult times. The story of her compassionate actions and the divine guidance she received became a symbol of the power of selfless giving.

This story emphasizes the importance of compassion, selflessness, and the role of Lord Ganesha in providing guidance and solutions when helping those in need.

Lord Ganesha and the Courageous Farmer

In a remote farming village, there lived a courageous farmer named Kavi. He was known for his determination and fearlessness in the face of challenges. Kavi's farm was the primary source of food for the entire village, and he took great pride in his work.

One year, the village faced a plague of locusts, threatening to devour the crops and cause famine. Kavi was determined to protect his farm and the livelihood of the villagers. He spent sleepless nights devising strategies to fend off the locusts.

As the locusts descended upon the village, Kavi turned to Lord Ganesha for guidance and assistance. He promised to stand firm and protect his land, even if it meant personal sacrifice. Kavi sought Ganesha's blessings to find a way to safeguard the crops.

Touched by Kavi's courage and dedication to his community, Lord Ganesha appeared before him in the form of a scarecrow. Ganesha explained how to create a unique scarecrow using brightly colored clothing, mirrors, and bells to scare away the locusts.

Kavi followed Ganesha's guidance and created the scarecrow as instructed. The unique and vibrant scarecrow was placed in the center of his farm. As the locusts approached, the mirrors and bells reflected the sunlight, creating a dazzling display that frightened the insects away.

Kavi's innovative scarecrow protected his farm, and the village was saved from the locust threat. The story of Kavi's courage and the divine guidance he received became an example of how determination and creativity can overcome even the most daunting challenges.

This story underscores the importance of courage, creativity, and the role of Lord Ganesha in providing guidance and solutions during times of crisis.

Lord Ganesha and the Grateful Sculptor

In a quaint town, there lived a talented sculptor named Alok. He was known for his exceptional skill in crafting exquisite idols of deities, including Lord Ganesha. Alok's work was highly sought after by devotees from all around the region.

One year, as Alok prepared for a grand festival dedicated to Lord Ganesha, he faced a challenge. His beloved sculpting tools, which had been passed down through generations, were stolen. Without these tools, he was unable to create the beautiful idol he had envisioned for the festival.

Alok was devastated and didn't know how to proceed. He turned to Lord Ganesha for guidance and assistance, promising to create a masterpiece if he could recover his stolen tools.

Touched by Alok's dedication to his craft and devotion to Lord Ganesha, the deity appeared before him. Ganesha handed Alok a small, unassuming chisel and encouraged him to begin sculpting with it.

Alok, despite his initial doubts, started to work with the chisel. To his amazement, he discovered that the chisel was no ordinary tool. It allowed him to create the most intricate and detailed idol he had ever made.

Alok's masterpiece for the Ganesha festival was a sight to behold, admired by all who saw it. It was a testimony to the divine guidance he had received and his unwavering determination to create art despite adversity.

The story of Alok's gratitude and the divine intervention in recovering his stolen tools became an inspiration to those who faced challenges. It emphasized the idea that dedication and creativity can overcome obstacles, with the support of faith and devotion.

This story highlights the importance of perseverance, creativity, and the role of Lord Ganesha in providing solutions and guidance during difficult times.

Lord Ganesha and the Compassionate Teacher

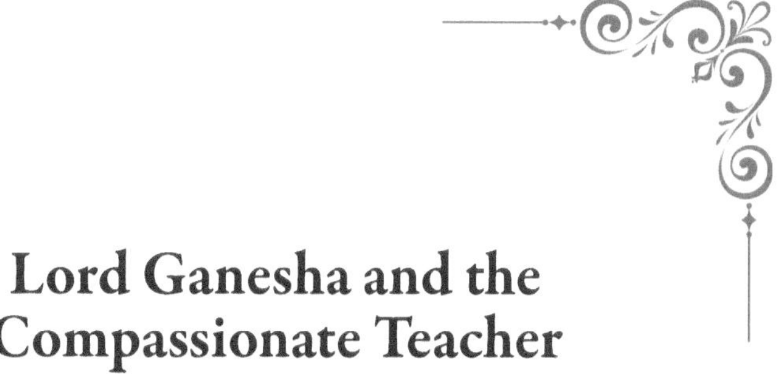

In a quiet village, there lived a dedicated teacher named Priya. She had a small school where she provided education to the children of the village, many of whom came from underprivileged families.

One year, the school faced a financial crisis, and Priya struggled to provide the necessary educational materials and resources for her students. She was determined to continue providing quality education, despite the challenges.

Priya turned to Lord Ganesha for guidance and assistance, praying for a solution to support her school and her students. She promised to do everything in her power to provide the best education to the children, regardless of the financial constraints.

Touched by Priya's dedication to her students and her commitment to education, Lord Ganesha appeared before her in the form of a scholar. He handed Priya a book of ancient wisdom and knowledge, which contained innovative teaching methods and a unique curriculum.

Priya embraced Ganesha's gift and began implementing the new curriculum in her school. The students were captivated by the innovative teaching methods and quickly started to excel in their studies.

The success of Priya's school, using the knowledge and methods provided by Lord Ganesha, became a testament to the power of education and the impact it could have on the lives of the children.

Priya continued to provide quality education to the underprivileged children, and her school became a beacon of hope and opportunity in the village. The story of her commitment and the divine guidance she received inspired others to prioritize education as a means of uplifting the community.

This story underscores the importance of education, dedication, and the role of Lord Ganesha in providing solutions and guidance in the pursuit of knowledge and betterment of society.

Lord Ganesha and the
Joyful Weaver

In a quaint village, there lived a skilled weaver named Maya. She was known for her exceptional ability to craft intricate and colorful textiles, which were highly valued by the villagers. Maya's creations were not only beautiful but also filled with positive energy and joy.

One year, the village faced a gloomy period, as heavy rains had caused flooding and disrupted daily life. People were struggling to find hope and happiness during these challenging times.

Maya, determined to bring positivity back to the village, turned to Lord Ganesha for guidance and assistance. She prayed for inspiration to create a weaving that would infuse joy into the hearts of the villagers, promising to share her creation with the entire community.

Touched by Maya's dedication and her desire to uplift the spirits of the villagers, Lord Ganesha appeared before her. He provided her with a unique combination of colorful threads that seemed to emit a radiant glow.

Maya used the special threads to create a weaving that depicted scenes of happiness, celebrations, and vibrant festivals. The weaving was filled with joy, and when people looked at it, they couldn't help but smile.

Maya displayed her creation in the village square, where it became a source of inspiration and positivity for the villagers. They found solace in the weaving, reminding them that joy could be found even in difficult times.

The story of Maya's dedication and the divine inspiration she received became a symbol of the power of art and creativity to bring happiness and hope to a community.

This story underscores the importance of art, positivity, and the role of Lord Ganesha in providing inspiration and solutions to uplift the spirits of those facing challenges.

Lord Ganesha and the
Dedicated Healer

In a remote village, there lived a dedicated healer named Anika. She was known for her exceptional skills in using herbal remedies and natural treatments to cure ailments. Anika's compassionate care had helped countless villagers recover from various illnesses.

One year, the village faced a health crisis as a severe epidemic spread throughout the region. Anika worked tirelessly to treat the sick and comfort the afflicted, often putting her own well-being at risk.

Despite her dedication, the epidemic continued to challenge her healing abilities. Anika turned to Lord Ganesha for guidance and assistance, praying for a solution to alleviate the suffering in the village. She promised to continue providing her healing services to the best of her abilities, even if it meant personal sacrifice.

Touched by Anika's unwavering commitment to her patients and her determination to help those in need, Lord Ganesha appeared before her. He provided her with a unique herbal remedy, a combination of rare ingredients that had powerful curative properties.

Anika used the remedy on her patients, and it proved to be highly effective in treating the epidemic. The village began to recover, and the once-ailing villagers regained their health and strength.

The story of Anika's dedication and the divine guidance she received became an inspiration to those who faced health challenges. It emphasized the importance of compassion, dedication, and the role of Lord Ganesha in providing solutions during times of illness and adversity.

This story highlights the significance of healing, compassion, and the belief that divine assistance can lead to solutions that alleviate suffering and bring relief to those in need.

Lord Ganesha and the
Diligent Farmer

In a serene countryside, there lived a diligent farmer named Ravi. He was known for his tireless work in cultivating the land, ensuring that the village had a constant supply of fresh, nutritious produce.

One year, a severe drought affected the region, leaving the land parched and the crops withering. The villagers, who depended on Ravi's farm for their livelihood, were filled with despair as their food sources dwindled.

Ravi refused to give in to the challenges posed by the drought. He continued to till the land and pray for rain, even though the skies remained clear. Ravi turned to Lord Ganesha, seeking guidance and assistance in bringing much-needed rain to the village. He promised to share his harvest with those in need, no matter the outcome.

Touched by Ravi's unwavering dedication and his commitment to the well-being of the villagers, Lord Ganesha appeared before him. He provided Ravi with a small clay idol and instructed him to perform a special ritual to invoke the rain.

Ravi followed Ganesha's guidance, and the entire village joined him in the rain-invoking ritual. They placed the clay idol in the center of the field, and with devotion in their hearts, they prayed for rain.

To everyone's amazement, dark clouds began to form in the sky. Rain started to fall, and the land was nourished, bringing relief to the parched earth. The villagers were overjoyed as they witnessed the power of their collective faith.

Ravi's farm thrived, and he shared his abundant harvest with the villagers. The story of Ravi's dedication and the divine intervention of Lord Ganesha became a symbol of the importance of perseverance, faith, and the belief that challenges can be overcome through unity and devotion.

This story emphasizes the significance of dedication, collective faith, and the role of Lord Ganesha in providing solutions during times of adversity, particularly in sustaining the land and livelihoods.

Lord Ganesha and the
Generous Potter

In a quiet village, there lived a generous potter named Suresh. He was known for his exceptional skills in crafting exquisite clay pots and other earthenware. Suresh's creations were not only beautiful but also highly durable and practical, earning him the admiration of the villagers.

One year, the village faced a shortage of clean drinking water, as their existing wells had run dry due to a prolonged dry season. The villagers were struggling to access a reliable source of fresh water.

Suresh, determined to help his community, turned to Lord Ganesha for guidance and assistance. He prayed for a solution to provide clean drinking water to the villagers, promising to use his pottery skills to benefit the entire community.

Touched by Suresh's selflessness and his commitment to the well-being of the villagers, Lord Ganesha appeared before him. Ganesha provided him with a design for a unique clay water filter that could purify even the murkiest water, making it safe to drink.

Suresh used Ganesha's design to create clay water filters, which were distributed to the villagers. The filters worked wonders, purifying the water and making it safe to drink. The villagers were relieved to have access to clean and healthy water once again.

Suresh's dedication and the divine guidance he received became a symbol of the power of generosity and community service. It emphasized the importance of selflessness and the role of Lord Ganesha in providing solutions to address the basic needs of a community.

This story underscores the significance of generosity, community service, and the belief that divine guidance can lead to solutions that benefit the well-being of an entire community.

Lord Ganesha and the
Resilient Fisher

In a coastal fishing village, there lived a resilient fisherman named Arjun. He was known for his unwavering determination and his deep connection to the sea. Arjun had faced numerous challenges, including storms and dangerous tides, but he never gave up on his trade.

One year, the village faced an economic crisis due to a decline in fish catches. The livelihood of the fishermen was threatened, and many were struggling to provide for their families. Arjun, despite the hardships, continued to cast his nets into the sea every day.

Arjun turned to Lord Ganesha for guidance and assistance, praying for a solution to restore the abundance of fish in the sea and revitalize the fishing industry. He promised to share his catch with those who were less fortunate, even if it meant personal sacrifice.

Touched by Arjun's resilience and his dedication to his fellow fishermen, Lord Ganesha appeared before him. Ganesha provided him with an ancient fisherman's chant, which, when recited daily, would bring good fortune and plentiful catches.

Arjun diligently recited the chant and shared it with his fellow fishermen. As they began to recite it together, a transformation occurred. The sea seemed to respond, and the fish returned in great numbers.

The fishing industry flourished, and the village once again thrived. Arjun and his fellow fishermen shared their catch with those who were in need, ensuring that no one went hungry.

The story of Arjun's resilience and the divine intervention of Lord Ganesha became a symbol of the power of determination and unity in the face of adversity. It emphasized the importance of working together for the common good and the role of Lord Ganesha in providing solutions during challenging times.

This story underscores the significance of resilience, unity, and the belief that divine assistance can lead to solutions that benefit the well-being of a community, particularly in sustaining livelihoods.

Lord Ganesha and the Devoted Scribe

In an ancient temple town, there lived a devoted scribe named Vikram. He was known for his meticulous skills in transcribing sacred texts and preserving the knowledge of the temple's rituals and traditions.

One year, the temple faced a dire situation. The main scriptural texts, which were central to the temple's practices, were damaged due to unforeseen circumstances. The loss of these texts had the potential to disrupt the temple's rituals and the spiritual life of the community.

Vikram, dedicated to preserving the sacred knowledge, turned to Lord Ganesha for guidance and assistance. He prayed for a solution to restore the damaged texts and promised to continue his role in maintaining the temple's traditions.

Touched by Vikram's devotion and his commitment to preserving the temple's knowledge, Lord Ganesha appeared before him. Ganesha provided Vikram with a vision of a hidden library within the temple that contained ancient scrolls with the missing texts.

With Ganesha's guidance, Vikram discovered the hidden library and the ancient scrolls. He meticulously transcribed the texts and restored the temple's knowledge, ensuring that the rituals and traditions continued without interruption.

The story of Vikram's dedication and the divine guidance he received became a symbol of the power of knowledge preservation and the importance of continuity in spiritual practices. It emphasized the significance of devotion and the role of Lord Ganesha in providing solutions to maintain sacred traditions.

This story underscores the importance of knowledge preservation, devotion, and the belief that divine intervention can lead to solutions that safeguard spiritual traditions.

Lord Ganesha and the
Humble Potter

In a serene village, there lived a humble potter named Parvati. She was known for her simplicity and her ability to craft basic yet functional clay pots and utensils. The villagers valued her creations for their durability and practicality.

One year, the village faced a severe shortage of food containers and cookware. The existing pots and pans were worn out, and many families struggled to cook and store their meals. Parvati, despite her modest means, continued to create clay pots to meet the needs of the villagers.

Parvati turned to Lord Ganesha for guidance and assistance, praying for a solution to provide enough pots and utensils for the entire village. She promised to use her pottery skills to benefit the community, even if it meant personal sacrifice.

Touched by Parvati's humility and her commitment to the well-being of the villagers, Lord Ganesha appeared before her. Ganesha provided her with a special technique to create clay pots more efficiently, allowing her to craft a greater number of utensils with the same amount of clay.

Parvati embraced Ganesha's guidance and used the new technique to create a surplus of clay pots and utensils. She distributed them to the villagers, ensuring that every family had enough to cook and store their meals.

The story of Parvati's humility and the divine intervention of Lord Ganesha became a symbol of the power of simplicity and practicality. It emphasized the importance of community support and the role of Lord Ganesha in providing solutions to address the basic needs of a community.

This story underscores the significance of simplicity, community support, and the belief that divine guidance can lead to solutions that benefit the well-being of an entire community, particularly in sustaining daily life.

Lord Ganesha and the
Resourceful Farmer

In a rural farming community, there lived a resourceful farmer named Deepak. He was known for his ability to adapt to changing circumstances and find innovative solutions to agricultural challenges. Deepak's farm was essential to the village's food supply.

One year, the village faced a severe infestation of crop-eating insects, threatening the livelihood of the farmers and the food source for the entire community. Deepak, undeterred by the adversity, sought to protect his crops and find a solution.

Deepak turned to Lord Ganesha for guidance and assistance, praying for a solution to save his crops from the infestation. He promised to continue using his resourcefulness to benefit the community, even if it meant personal sacrifice.

Touched by Deepak's resourcefulness and his commitment to the well-being of the community, Lord Ganesha appeared before him. Ganesha provided Deepak with a natural pesticide formula, using a combination of herbs and plants that would deter the insects.

Deepak used Ganesha's natural pesticide formula on his crops, and it proved to be highly effective in repelling the insects. His farm was saved, and he shared the formula with other farmers in the village to protect their crops as well.

The story of Deepak's resourcefulness and the divine intervention of Lord Ganesha became a symbol of the power of adaptability and innovation in the face of agricultural challenges. It emphasized the importance of community support and the role of Lord Ganesha in providing solutions to protect essential resources.

This story underscores the significance of resourcefulness, community cooperation, and the belief that divine guidance can lead to solutions that safeguard essential resources for a community.

Lord Ganesha and the Grateful Herbalist

In a tranquil forest village, there lived a skilled herbalist named Nalini. She was known for her deep knowledge of medicinal herbs and her ability to heal various ailments. Nalini's remedies were sought after by villagers and travelers who visited her to seek relief from their health issues.

One year, a severe epidemic gripped the village, and Nalini's herbal remedies were in high demand. She worked tirelessly to treat the sick and alleviate their suffering, often traveling deep into the forest to gather rare herbs for her treatments.

Despite her dedication, the epidemic continued to challenge her healing abilities. Nalini turned to Lord Ganesha for guidance and assistance, praying for a solution to heal the villagers and promising to continue her work in preserving the health of the community.

Touched by Nalini's expertise and her commitment to the well-being of the villagers, Lord Ganesha appeared before her. He provided her with knowledge of a unique healing herb hidden deep within the forest, which possessed miraculous curative properties.

Nalini ventured into the forest, guided by Ganesha's wisdom, and located the rare herb. She used it to create a potent remedy that proved highly effective in treating the epidemic. The villagers began to recover, and hope was restored.

The story of Nalini's expertise and the divine guidance she received became a symbol of the power of herbal medicine and the importance of dedicated healers. It emphasized the significance of compassion and the role of Lord Ganesha in providing solutions to alleviate suffering during times of illness and crisis.

This story underscores the importance of herbal medicine, compassion, and the belief that divine intervention can lead to solutions that preserve the health and well-being of a community.

Lord Ganesha and the
Resilient Blacksmith

In a bustling market town, there lived a resilient blacksmith named Raghav. He was known for his exceptional skills in crafting sturdy tools and implements, which were highly sought after by farmers and artisans in the region.

One year, the town faced a severe shortage of iron, and the prices of metal tools soared, leaving many struggling to afford the essential equipment for their work. Raghav, undeterred by the challenges, continued to create iron tools to meet the needs of the community.

Raghav turned to Lord Ganesha for guidance and assistance, praying for a solution to ensure a steady supply of iron for his blacksmithing work. He promised to use his skills to support the livelihoods of the townspeople, even if it meant personal sacrifice.

Touched by Raghav's resilience and his commitment to the well-being of the community, Lord Ganesha appeared before him. Ganesha provided him with a vision of an iron-rich ore deposit hidden in the nearby hills.

Raghav, guided by Ganesha's vision, ventured into the hills and located the iron ore deposit. He established a sustainable mining operation, ensuring a steady supply of iron for his blacksmithing work and for the community.

The story of Raghav's resilience and the divine intervention of Lord Ganesha became a symbol of the power of perseverance and innovation in the face of resource scarcity. It emphasized the importance of community support and the role of Lord Ganesha in providing solutions to ensure the availability of essential resources.

This story underscores the significance of resourcefulness, community cooperation, and the belief that divine guidance can lead to solutions that support the livelihoods of a community.

Lord Ganesha and the
Wise Farmer

In a serene countryside, there lived a wise farmer named Keshav. He was known for his deep understanding of the land and his ability to produce bountiful harvests year after year. Keshav's farm was a source of sustenance and prosperity for the entire village.

One year, the region faced a series of unpredictable weather patterns, which left many farmers struggling with failed crops. Keshav, however, continued to tend to his land with patience and wisdom.

Keshav turned to Lord Ganesha for guidance and assistance, praying for a solution to navigate the uncertainty of the weather and ensure the well-being of the village. He promised to share his knowledge and farming techniques with his fellow farmers, even if it meant personal sacrifice.

Touched by Keshav's wisdom and his commitment to the welfare of the community, Lord Ganesha appeared before him. Ganesha shared insights on sustainable farming practices that would allow Keshav to adapt to changing weather patterns and improve the yield of his crops.

Keshav embraced Ganesha's guidance and began implementing the sustainable farming practices. He also shared this knowledge with his fellow farmers, helping them adapt to the unpredictable weather and improve their own harvests.

The story of Keshav's wisdom and the divine guidance he received became a symbol of the power of knowledge and sustainability in the face of environmental challenges. It emphasized the importance of community support and the role of Lord Ganesha in providing solutions to ensure the well-being of the land and the people.

This story underscores the significance of wisdom, community cooperation, and the belief that divine guidance can lead to solutions that support the prosperity of a community, particularly in sustaining agriculture and livelihoods.

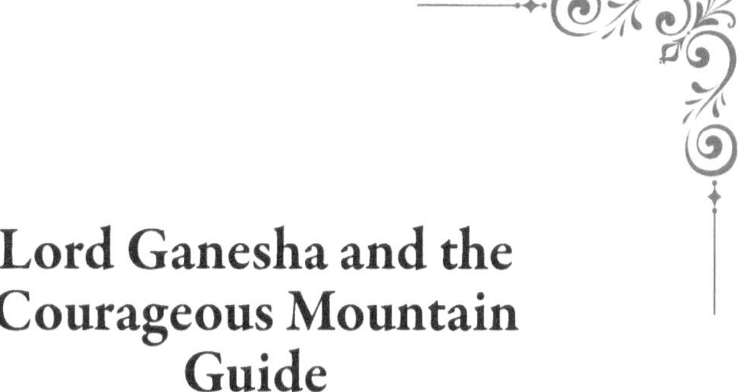

Lord Ganesha and the Courageous Mountain Guide

In a remote mountain village, there lived a courageous guide named Suman. He was known for his extraordinary skills in leading treks and expeditions through the treacherous mountain terrain. Suman's guidance was highly valued by travelers and adventurers who sought to explore the majestic peaks.

One year, a group of travelers found themselves stranded in a dangerous situation during a harsh winter storm in the mountains. Suman, unfazed by the challenges, risked his life to ensure the safety of the travelers, leading them to a hidden mountain shelter.

Suman turned to Lord Ganesha for guidance and assistance, praying for a solution to protect the travelers from the harsh elements and ensure their survival. He promised to continue his role as a guide and protector of those who ventured into the mountains, even if it meant personal sacrifice.

Touched by Suman's courage and his commitment to the safety of the travelers, Lord Ganesha appeared before him. Ganesha provided Suman with a vision of an ancient cave deep within the mountains, which could serve as a safe haven during storms and adverse conditions.

Suman guided the travelers to the hidden cave, where they found shelter from the storm. The cave provided warmth and protection, allowing the travelers to survive the harsh weather until they could safely descend the mountains.

The story of Suman's courage and the divine intervention of Lord Ganesha became a symbol of the power of bravery and protection in the face of nature's challenges. It emphasized the importance of guiding and safeguarding others and the role of Lord Ganesha in providing solutions to ensure the well-being of adventurers.

This story underscores the significance of courage, protection, and the belief that divine guidance can lead to solutions that ensure the safety and survival of those who venture into the natural world.

Lord Ganesha and the
Diligent Potter

In a quaint village, there lived a diligent potter named Maya. She was known for her unwavering commitment to creating finely crafted clay pots and figurines. Maya's creations were not only functional but also served as works of art.

One year, a series of misfortunes struck the village, leaving many families without a source of income. Maya, however, continued to create her pottery with dedication and care, hoping to uplift the spirits of the villagers.

Maya turned to Lord Ganesha for guidance and assistance, praying for a solution to help the struggling families in the village. She promised to use her pottery skills to generate opportunities for employment, even if it meant personal sacrifice.

Touched by Maya's diligence and her commitment to the well-being of the villagers, Lord Ganesha appeared before her. Ganesha provided her with a vision of creating a pottery workshop that would employ members of the community in crafting and selling pottery.

Maya embraced Ganesha's guidance and established the pottery workshop in the village. She trained local artisans in pottery-making techniques, and the workshop became a source of employment for many families. The pottery crafted there gained recognition, attracting buyers from other villages.

The story of Maya's diligence and the divine intervention of Lord Ganesha became a symbol of the power of hard work and community support in the face of economic hardships. It emphasized the importance of generating opportunities for employment and the role of Lord Ganesha in providing solutions to uplift the livelihoods of a community.

This story underscores the significance of diligence, community cooperation, and the belief that divine guidance can lead to solutions that create economic opportunities and well-being for a community.

Lord Ganesha and the Harmonious Musicians

In a vibrant town, there lived a group of talented musicians known for their exceptional skills in playing traditional instruments. They created beautiful melodies that resonated through the town, bringing joy to all who heard their music.

One year, the town faced a discord among the musicians, leading to the cessation of their performances. The absence of their harmonious music left the townspeople disheartened and longing for the melodies they once enjoyed.

The musicians turned to Lord Ganesha for guidance and assistance, praying for a solution to restore their harmony and bring back the joy of their music to the town. They promised to put aside their differences and work together for the well-being of the community.

Touched by the musicians' dedication to their art and their commitment to the community, Lord Ganesha appeared before them. Ganesha inspired them to combine their diverse musical talents and styles, creating a fusion of melodies that were unique and enchanting.

The musicians embraced Ganesha's guidance and worked together to create this fusion of musical styles. When they performed their harmonious compositions, the town was filled with the joy of their enchanting music once again.

The story of the harmonious musicians and the divine intervention of Lord Ganesha became a symbol of the power of unity and collaboration in the face of discord. It emphasized the significance of working together for the well-being of the community and the role of Lord Ganesha in providing solutions that restore harmony.

This story underscores the importance of unity, community cooperation, and the belief that divine guidance can lead to solutions that bring joy and well-being to a community through the arts.

Lord Ganesha and the
Kind Village Healer

In a tranquil village, there lived a kind-hearted healer named Preeti. She was known for her ability to provide remedies for various ailments and injuries using natural herbs and healing techniques. Preeti's compassionate care was valued by the villagers.

One year, an epidemic began to spread throughout the village, causing illness and suffering among the residents. Preeti, driven by her compassion, worked tirelessly to treat the sick and offer comfort to those in distress.

Preeti turned to Lord Ganesha for guidance and assistance, praying for a solution to alleviate the suffering caused by the epidemic. She promised to continue her role as a healer and support the well-being of the village, even if it meant personal sacrifice.

Touched by Preeti's kindness and her dedication to the well-being of the villagers, Lord Ganesha appeared before her. Ganesha provided her with insights into a unique herbal remedy that could effectively treat the epidemic and alleviate the symptoms of the afflicted.

Preeti used Ganesha's guidance to create the herbal remedy, and it proved to be highly effective in treating the epidemic. She distributed the remedy to the villagers, and the epidemic's impact began to wane. Preeti continued to care for those in need, ensuring their recovery and well-being.

The story of Preeti's kindness and the divine intervention of Lord Ganesha became a symbol of the power of compassion and the importance of healing during times of illness and suffering. It emphasized the significance of community support and the role of Lord Ganesha in providing solutions to alleviate pain and distress.

This story underscores the importance of kindness, community cooperation, and the belief that divine guidance can lead to solutions that bring relief and well-being to a community during times of hardship.

Lord Ganesha and the Devoted Artist

In a bustling artistic community, there lived a devoted artist named Aarav. He was known for his exceptional talent in creating intricate sculptures and paintings, which were admired for their beauty and creativity.

One year, a series of unfortunate events left Aarav struggling to find inspiration for his artwork. His creative block led to a halt in his artistic endeavors, leaving the community longing for his masterpieces.

Aarav turned to Lord Ganesha for guidance and assistance, praying for a solution to rekindle his artistic inspiration and bring his creations back to life. He promised to continue using his artistic skills to inspire and uplift the spirits of those who admired his work.

Touched by Aarav's dedication to his art and his commitment to sharing beauty with the community, Lord Ganesha appeared before him. Ganesha provided him with visions of breathtaking landscapes, inspiring scenes, and intricate designs that served as a wellspring of inspiration.

Aarav embraced Ganesha's guidance and embarked on a journey to create art based on the visions he received. His artwork captured the beauty and awe-inspiring scenes that he had seen in his visions, delighting the community with his renewed creativity.

The story of Aarav's devotion and the divine intervention of Lord Ganesha became a symbol of the power of artistic inspiration and the importance of sharing beauty through art. It emphasized the significance of creativity and the role of Lord Ganesha in providing solutions to revive the spirits of a community through artistic expression.

This story underscores the importance of creativity, community appreciation of art, and the belief that divine guidance can lead to solutions that rekindle the creative spirit and bring joy to a community through the arts.

Lord Ganesha and the Devoted Gardener

In a serene garden, there lived a devoted gardener named Neelam. She was known for her remarkable ability to cultivate diverse and lush plant life that filled the garden with vibrant colors and sweet fragrances. Neelam's garden was a source of tranquility and joy for all who visited.

One year, a severe infestation of pests threatened to destroy the garden's delicate ecosystem. Neelam, undeterred by the challenge, continued to tend to her plants with care and love, seeking a way to protect her beloved garden.

Neelam turned to Lord Ganesha for guidance and assistance, praying for a solution to rid her garden of the infestation and restore its natural beauty. She promised to continue her role as a caretaker of the garden and share her knowledge with others, even if it meant personal sacrifice.

Touched by Neelam's devotion and her commitment to the well-being of the garden, Lord Ganesha appeared before her. Ganesha provided her with insights into natural and environmentally friendly methods to combat the infestation, ensuring that the garden would flourish once again.

Neelam embraced Ganesha's guidance and implemented the eco-friendly methods in her garden. With time and patience, she successfully rid the garden of pests and restored its beauty. She also shared her knowledge with other gardeners, helping them protect their gardens in a sustainable manner.

The story of Neelam's devotion and the divine intervention of Lord Ganesha became a symbol of the power of dedication and sustainability in the face of challenges to the natural world. It emphasized the importance of community support and the role of Lord Ganesha in providing solutions to nurture and protect the environment.

This story underscores the significance of devotion to nature, community cooperation, and the belief that divine guidance can lead to solutions that restore the beauty and well-being of the natural world for the benefit of all.

Lord Ganesha and the
Generous Merchant

In a thriving marketplace, there lived a generous merchant named Harish. He was known for his willingness to support charitable causes and help those less fortunate. Harish's acts of kindness made him a respected figure in the community.

One year, a significant economic downturn affected the marketplace, leaving many families in financial distress. Harish, however, continued to conduct his business and sought ways to assist those facing hardship.

Harish turned to Lord Ganesha for guidance and assistance, praying for a solution to alleviate the financial struggles of the marketplace and provide support to the affected families. He promised to continue using his business success to support the well-being of the community, even if it meant personal sacrifice.

Touched by Harish's generosity and his commitment to the community's welfare, Lord Ganesha appeared before him. Ganesha provided him with innovative ideas to adapt his business and create opportunities for the struggling families to regain their financial stability.

Harish embraced Ganesha's guidance and implemented the innovative business strategies. He offered employment and financial support to many affected families, helping them rebuild their livelihoods and recover from the economic downturn.

The story of Harish's generosity and the divine intervention of Lord Ganesha became a symbol of the power of charity and community support in the face of economic challenges. It emphasized the importance of business innovation and the role of Lord Ganesha in providing solutions to uplift the financial well-being of a community.

This story underscores the significance of generosity, community cooperation, and the belief that divine guidance can lead to solutions that restore economic stability and well-being for a community during difficult economic times.

Lord Ganesha and the
Determined Craftsman

In a quaint village, there lived a determined craftsman named Rajat. He was known for his exceptional craftsmanship in creating intricate jewelry and ornaments, which were cherished by those who wore them. Rajat's creations were considered priceless works of art.

One year, a series of unfortunate events left Rajat unable to find the precious gemstones he needed for his jewelry designs. Undeterred by the challenge, he continued to search for alternative materials and methods to create his intricate pieces.

Rajat turned to Lord Ganesha for guidance and assistance, praying for a solution to continue his craft and inspire others in the art of jewelry making. He promised to share his knowledge with aspiring craftsmen, even if it meant personal sacrifice.

Touched by Rajat's determination and his commitment to the art of jewelry making, Lord Ganesha appeared before him. Ganesha provided him with insights into using unique and unconventional materials to create jewelry that was equally stunning and original.

Rajat embraced Ganesha's guidance and began experimenting with the unconventional materials. He not only continued his own jewelry craft but also shared his knowledge with aspiring craftsmen, sparking a new wave of creativity in the village.

The story of Rajat's determination and the divine intervention of Lord Ganesha became a symbol of the power of creativity and resourcefulness in the face of material scarcity. It emphasized the importance of artistic mentorship and the role of Lord Ganesha in providing solutions to nurture the crafts and arts.

This story underscores the significance of determination, community support, and the belief that divine guidance can lead to solutions that encourage creativity and artistic expression within a community.

Lord Ganesha and the Compassionate Teacher

In a small village, there lived a compassionate teacher named Kavita. She was known for her dedication to educating the village children and instilling in them a love for learning. Kavita's teaching was celebrated for its ability to inspire young minds.

One year, a shortage of educational materials and resources threatened to disrupt the children's education. Kavita, undeterred by the challenge, continued to teach using innovative methods and sought ways to provide her students with the knowledge they deserved.

Kavita turned to Lord Ganesha for guidance and assistance, praying for a solution to ensure that her students received a quality education and had access to necessary resources. She promised to continue her role as an educator and mentor, even if it meant personal sacrifice.

Touched by Kavita's compassion and her commitment to the education of the village children, Lord Ganesha appeared before her. Ganesha provided her with insights into creative and resourceful teaching methods that would help her make the most of limited resources and engage her students effectively.

Kavita embraced Ganesha's guidance and implemented the creative teaching methods. Her students flourished, and they developed a deeper love for learning. Kavita's innovative teaching style inspired other educators in the village, who also adopted these methods.

The story of Kavita's compassion and the divine intervention of Lord Ganesha became a symbol of the power of education and creative teaching in the face of resource constraints. It emphasized the importance of mentorship and the role of Lord Ganesha in providing solutions to nurture the young minds of a community.

This story underscores the significance of education, community support, and the belief that divine guidance can lead to solutions that ensure access to quality learning for the children of a community, no matter the challenges they may face.

Lord Ganesha and the
Caring Healer

In a remote village, there lived a caring healer named Sanjana. She was known for her selfless service in providing healthcare to the villagers, using traditional remedies and her knowledge of medicinal herbs. Sanjana's compassionate care made her a respected figure in the community.

One year, a severe outbreak of a mysterious illness afflicted the village, causing widespread fear and suffering. Sanjana, however, continued to treat the sick and sought ways to alleviate their pain and discomfort.

Sanjana turned to Lord Ganesha for guidance and assistance, praying for a solution to combat the mysterious illness and ensure the well-being of the villagers. She promised to continue her role as a healer and caretaker, even if it meant personal sacrifice.

Touched by Sanjana's care and her commitment to the welfare of the community, Lord Ganesha appeared before her. Ganesha provided her with insights into effective remedies and healing techniques that could provide relief to the afflicted villagers and contain the outbreak.

Sanjana embraced Ganesha's guidance and applied the remedies and techniques to treat the ill. Her compassionate care and the effectiveness of her treatments helped many villagers recover from the illness, and the outbreak was eventually brought under control.

The story of Sanjana's care and the divine intervention of Lord Ganesha became a symbol of the power of compassion and traditional healing methods in the face of a health crisis. It emphasized the importance of community support and the role of Lord Ganesha in providing solutions to ensure the well-being of a community during times of illness.

This story underscores the significance of compassion, community cooperation, and the belief that divine guidance can lead to solutions that bring relief and well-being to a community during health crises.

Lord Ganesha and the
Resourceful Blacksmith

In a bustling town, there lived a resourceful blacksmith named Arvind. He was known for his skill in crafting durable tools and equipment for the townsfolk, which helped them in their daily tasks. Arvind's dedication to his craft made him an essential figure in the community.

One year, a scarcity of metal resources threatened to disrupt the production of tools and equipment, leaving the townspeople without the essential items they needed. Arvind, undeterred by the challenge, continued to seek innovative ways to provide the community with the tools they required.

Arvind turned to Lord Ganesha for guidance and assistance, praying for a solution to overcome the scarcity of metal resources and ensure the townspeople had access to the tools they needed. He promised to continue his role as a blacksmith and share his resourceful techniques, even if it meant personal sacrifice.

Touched by Arvind's resourcefulness and his commitment to the well-being of the community, Lord Ganesha appeared before him. Ganesha provided him with insights into alternative materials and techniques that could be used to craft durable tools and equipment, even without an abundance of metal.

Arvind embraced Ganesha's guidance and began experimenting with alternative materials and techniques. He not only continued to supply the townsfolk with high-quality tools but also shared his knowledge with other craftsmen, helping them adapt to the new methods.

The story of Arvind's resourcefulness and the divine intervention of Lord Ganesha became a symbol of the power of innovation and adaptability in the face of material scarcity. It emphasized the importance of community support and the role of Lord Ganesha in providing solutions to ensure the well-being of a community.

This story underscores the significance of resourcefulness, community cooperation, and the belief that divine guidance can lead to solutions that provide essential tools and equipment for the well-being of a community during times of resource scarcity.

Conclusion

As the final pages of "Ganesha's Whispers" unfold, we witness the transformative power of wisdom and the auspicious beginnings that Lord Ganesha has bestowed upon our characters. The obstacles that once seemed insurmountable have been cleared, making way for new and profound journeys.

Ganesha's gentle whispers have not only removed hindrances but have also sown the seeds of enlightenment in the hearts of our protagonists. They stand on the threshold of a new chapter, armed with the divine wisdom imparted by the benevolent deity.

The tales of Ganesha's guidance have etched themselves into the very fabric of these characters' lives, leaving an indelible mark that transcends time and space. As the book draws to a close, readers are left with a sense of hope, resilience, and the belief that every ending is but a prelude to a new beginning.

Upcoming Books:

Book 2: "Krishna's Melodies: Harmonies of Love and Devotion"

- Prepare to be immersed in the enchanting world of Lord Krishna, where divine melodies weave harmonies of love and profound devotion. The playful and compassionate deity will guide characters through a symphony of experiences that resonate with the essence of divine love.

Book 3: "Ram's Odyssey: Epics of Sacrifice and Valor"

- Embark on an epic journey with Lord Ram, where sacrifice and valor take center stage. Characters will navigate intricate paths guided by the unwavering principles of righteousness, showcasing the triumph of good over evil in a tale of resilience and unwavering commitment.

As we bid farewell to Ganesha's wisdom, the anticipation for the forthcoming volumes grows. The Divine Trilogy promises to unfold rich narratives, timeless wisdom, and celestial adventures, inviting readers to delve deeper into the realms of Krishna and Ram. The journey continues, and the whispers of divinity echo through the pages, beckoning readers to explore the cosmic tales that await.

About the Author

Jignesh, a devoted project engineer during the day and an ardent writer at heart, possesses a unique blend of analytical prowess and creative finesse. His insatiable **love for storytelling** fuels his mission to unravel intricate topics in a way that captivates readers and makes learning an enchanting experience.

With a canvas of words, Jignesh weaves tales that bridge the chasm between complex concepts and everyday life, creating literary tapestries that entwine the profound with the practical. He believes in the power of storytelling to unlock the doors of understanding, inviting readers of all backgrounds to embark on a journey of knowledge and self-discovery.

Beyond the world of engineering, Jignesh's soul finds solace in the realm of literature and the art of expression. Each sentence he pens is crafted with passion and purpose, driven by the conviction that education should be an enjoyable voyage of curiosity and wonder.

When he is not immersed in the realm of storytelling, Jignesh can be found communing with nature's beauty, penning verses of poetry, or sharing cherished moments with loved ones. His unwavering commitment to both his professional career and creative pursuits reflects a harmonious balance between the logical and the imaginative.